Julia Rothman's
OCEAN
ANATOMY
ACTIVITY BOOK

FOR CURIOUS KIDS

YOU CAN FIND ALL THESE NATURAL THINGS IN THIS BOOK

_____

_____

_____

But first, how many of them can you identify before you turn the page? Write the names in the blanks. Give yourself a point for each one you know.

After you do all the puzzles, come back to this page and see how much you've learned. Give yourself another point for each blank you fill in.

_____

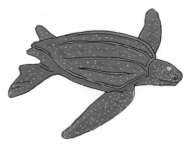

_____

SCORE BEFORE DOING BOOK	SCORE AFTER DOING WHOLE BOOK

Are you a BEACHCOMBER
or a CAPTAIN OF THE CURRENTS?

1-5 POINTS BEACHCOMBER
6-10 POINTS WAVE RIDER
11-15 POINTS NAUTICAL NERD
16-24 POINTS CAPTAIN OF THE CURRENTS

_____

_____

MEASURE THE SIZE

Use the measuring tape to figure out the approximate
size of each whale. Write your findings on the lines.

0   10   20   30   40   50   60   70

FEET

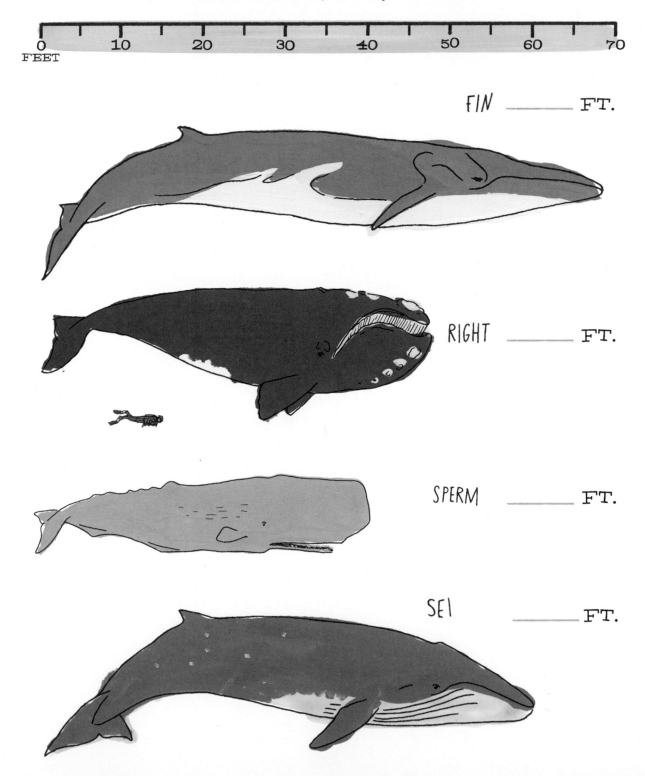

FIN _____ FT.

RIGHT _____ FT.

SPERM _____ FT.

SEI _____ FT.

4

Here are some smaller whales to measure, using a different measuring tape.
Use a real measuring tape to find out how tall you are. Draw yourself swimming
under the diver and see how you compare. Don't forget to add flippers!

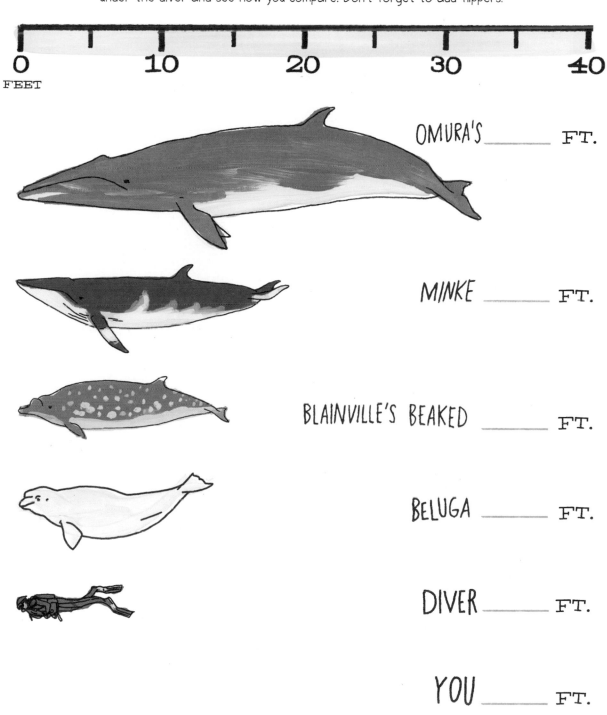

0   10   20   30   40
FEET

OMURA'S _____ FT.

MINKE _____ FT.

BLAINVILLE'S BEAKED _____ FT.

BELUGA _____ FT.

DIVER _____ FT.

YOU _____ FT.

Dolphin-ately Different

Dolphins and porpoises may look similar but there are some small differences when you look closely. See if you can find them and label the drawing with the descriptive words from the box below.

DOLPHIN

long beak	triangular dorsal fin	spade-shaped teeth	slender body
small mouth	curved dorsal fin	cone-shaped teeth	round body

PORPOISE

MAKE IT:
KINETIC SAND

Kinetic sand can be molded into all sorts of shapes. It has a squishy texture like wet sand that makes it lots of fun to play with. It's simple and inexpensive to make.

What You'll Need:

- 2½ cups of sand (You can use fine beach sand or garden sand or buy craft sand in various colors.)
- ½ cup cornstarch
- ½ cup cooking oil

1. Put the sand and cornstarch into a large bowl and mix them well with your hands or a spoon.

2. Pour the oil into the bowl and mix until the oil is evenly distributed. You don't want any oily spots or dry parts in the mixture.

3. Use your hands to make sea creatures or castles. Make shapes with molds or cookie cutters. Store your sand in an airtight container so you can use it over and over.

HOW TO DRAW A DOLPHIN

1. In pencil, sketch out a long oblong shape that tapers at the end.

2. Add a tail with two flukes or fins, and a rostrum, its beak-like snout.

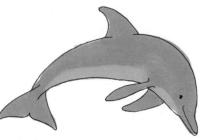

3. Next add two pectoral fins, and the dorsal fin on top.

4. Lastly, add an eye and mouth.

5. Go over your pencil lines in ink.

6. Add color if you wish.

Now You Try ↳

DOLPHIN

SECRET CODE

Nautical signal flags are used internationally for ship-to-ship communication. Each flag has a specific meaning. Can you decipher the coded message below using these flags?

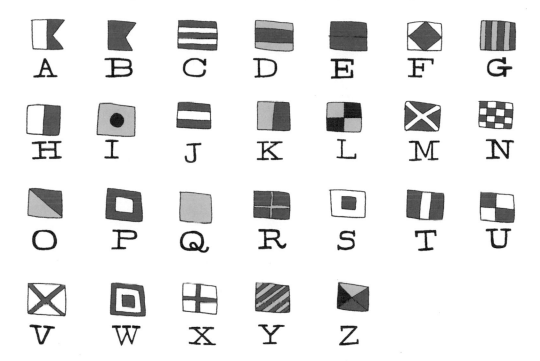

WHAT'S THE MESSAGE?

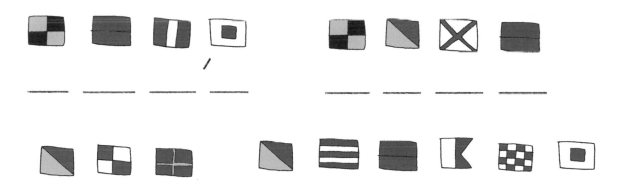

ALPHABETIC OCEAN

Can you think of things you can find in the ocean that start with every letter of the alphabet?
Three answers are filled in to get you started. Some letters might be really hard, but think creatively.

A _____

B _____

C _____

D _____

E _____

F _____

G _____

H _____

I _____

J _____

K _____

L _____

M _____

N _____

O _____

P _____

Q ____ quahog _____

R _____

S _____

T _____

U _____

V ____ vampire squid _____

W _____

X ____ X-ray fish _____

Y _____

Z _____

ANATOMY OF AN OCTOPUS

Write the number of each part in the corresponding line next to the description.

_____ **arm** flexible appendage covered in suckers
_____ **siphon** for breathing and propulsion through water
_____ **sucker** for gripping prey
_____ **mantle** bag-like body
_____ **eye** has a rectangular pupil

HOW TO DRAW A SQUID

1. Draw the first two shapes that make up the mantle and head.

2. Add the fins, eyes, and eight lines that will become the arms.

3. Finish the arms and add two tentacles.

4. Ink over the drawing and add tiny dots to represent the chromatophores (pigment-containing cells).

5. Add color. Squids have color-changing capabilities. They can go from brown to red to rainbow metallic.

Now You Try ↴

SQUID

HIGH TIDE

Tide zones host a wide variety of animals that are hardy enough to survive in constantly changing conditions. Study all the creatures on this page and then turn the page to see how many you remember.

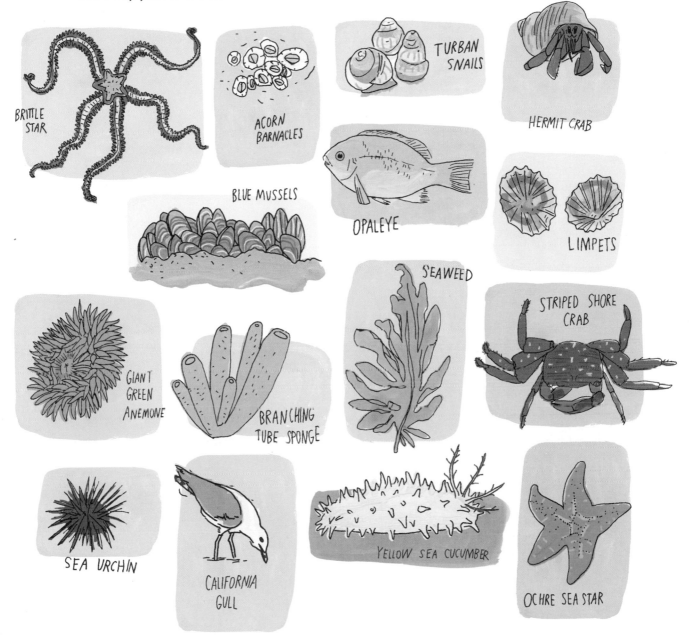

BRITTLE STAR

ACORN BARNACLES

TURBAN SNAILS

HERMIT CRAB

BLUE MUSSELS

OPALEYE

LIMPETS

GIANT GREEN ANEMONE

BRANCHING TUBE SPONGE

SEAWEED

STRIPED SHORE CRAB

SEA URCHIN

CALIFORNIA GULL

YELLOW SEA CUCUMBER

OCHRE SEA STAR

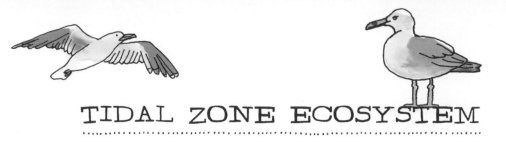

TIDAL ZONE ECOSYSTEM

Without flipping back to the previous page, see how many sea creature names you can fill in.

limpet
brittle star
striped shore crab
sea cucumber
turban snail
anemone
mussels
opaleye

sea urchins
gull
hermit crab
barnacles
seaweed
sponge
sea star

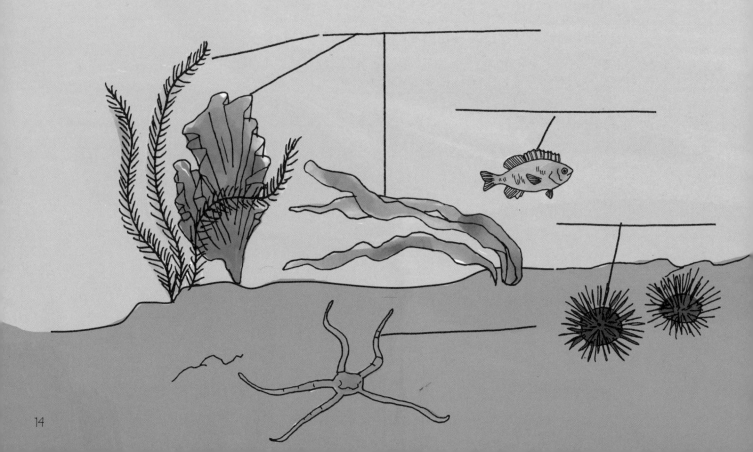

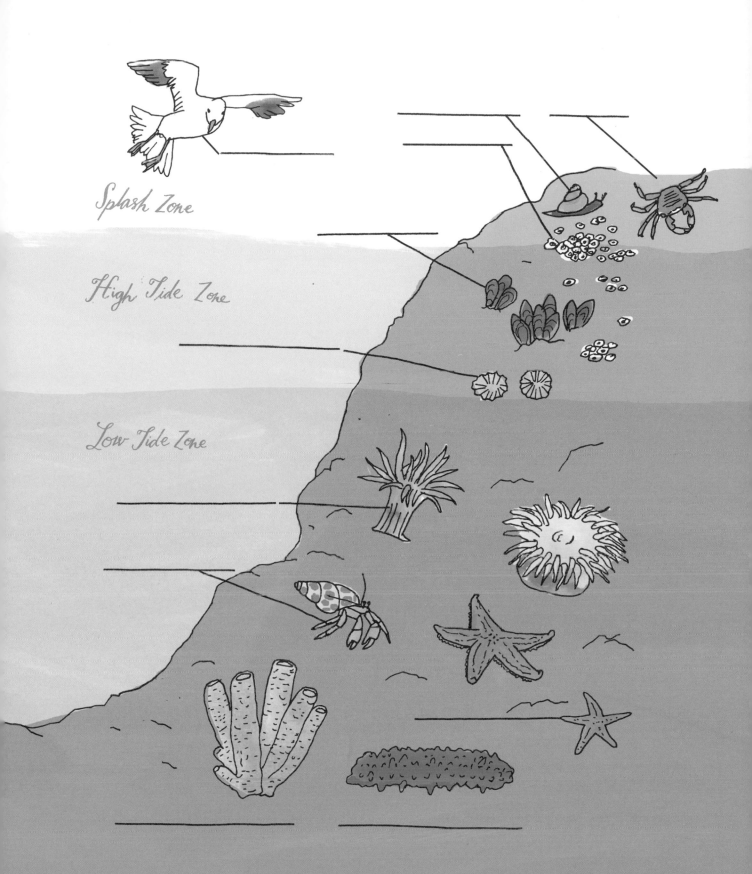

Splash Zone

High Tide Zone

Low Tide Zone

Hermit Crab Homes

Instead having of a full exoskeleton (a hard outer shell), hermit crabs must find a shell to protect their soft bodies. They slide their spiral hindquarters into the empty shells of marine snails or other invertebrates. As they grow, they have to move into larger shells.

Sometimes hermit crabs use aluminum cans, plastic containers, nut hulls, or hollow bits of wood instead of shells.

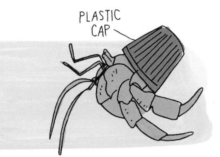

PLASTIC CAP

The hermit crabs below need to find new homes. Draw a shell for each one or use your imagination to come up with something that could protect them.

FEELING CRABBY?

Fill in the 4-by-4 grid so that all the letters of the word C-R-A-B appear only once in each row and once in each column.

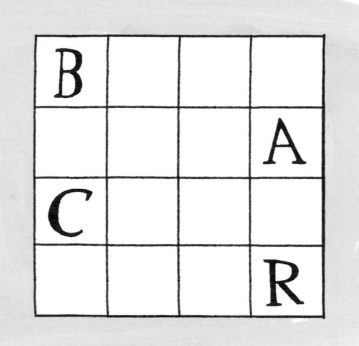

Crabs are crustaceans that have hard exoskeletons and 10 legs, including their claws. These crabs are missing some legs and claws. Can you draw the missing ones to match?

HARLEQUIN CRAB

BLUE CRAB

SNOW CRAB

GRAPH A BEACH

How much nature can you find on your next visit to the beach? Head to the shore and start recording what you see. Color in a square in the graph for each species (type) of shell, plant, fish, bird, or other animal you see. Use the blank lines for things you find that aren't on the list.

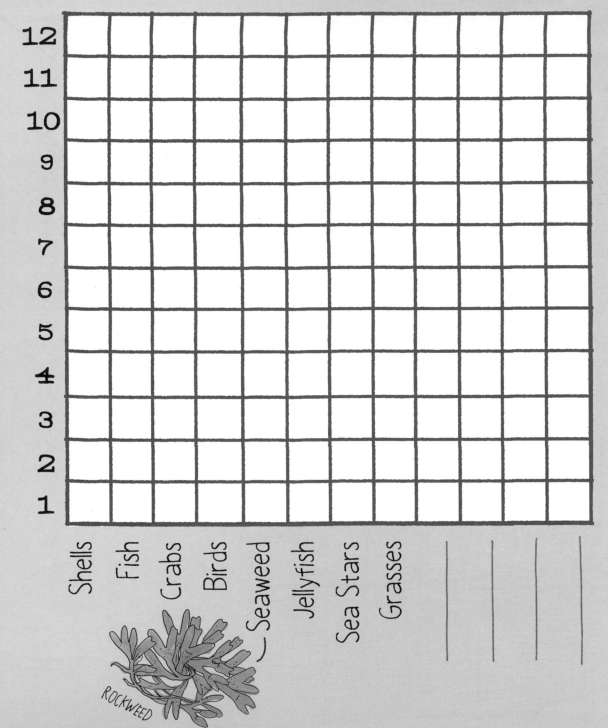

Number I Saw

12
11
10
9
8
7
6
5
4
3
2
1

Shells   Fish   Crabs   Birds   Seaweed   Jellyfish   Sea Stars   Grasses

ROCKWEED

SEA CREATURE SCRAMBLER

Can you unscramble the letters to figure out the names of these ocean
crawlers? Write the names in the spaces below each one.

rilkl

qudis

_ _ _ _ _ _ _ _

aes tsra

wons brca

_ _ _ _ _ _ _ _ _

reblost

optcosu

_ _ _ _ _ _ _ _ _ _

oonm nasil

clopsal

_ _ _ _ _ _ _ _ _ _ _

MY SHELL DISCOVERIES

Do you like looking for shells on the beach? There are so many different kinds to find. Use these pages to catalog the shells you see. Draw pictures of them or take photos to glue to the page.

PACIFIC
PINK
SCALLOP

PINK CONCH

WEST INDIAN
WORM SHELL

ROSE
PETAL
TELLIN

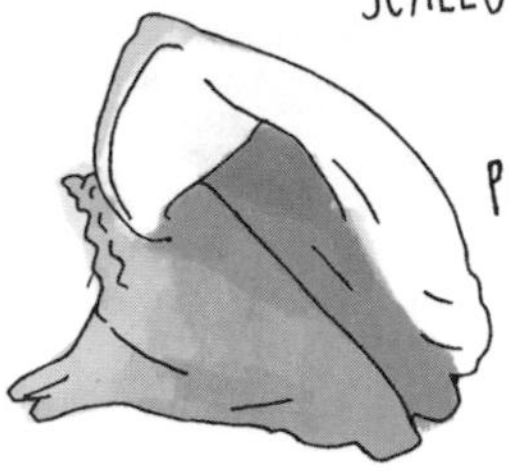

Date:

Kind of shell:

Notes:

Date:

Kind of shell:

Notes:

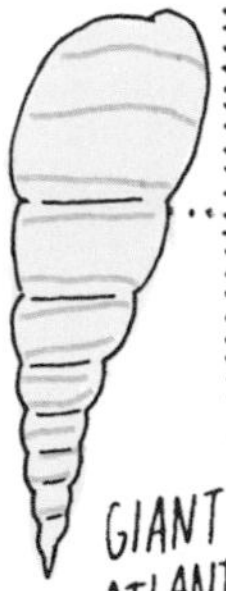

GIANT
ATLANTIC
PYRAM

Date:

Kind of shell:

Notes:

Date:

Kind of shell:

Notes:

COUE'S SPINDLE
SHELL

WHITE-SPOTTED
ENGINA

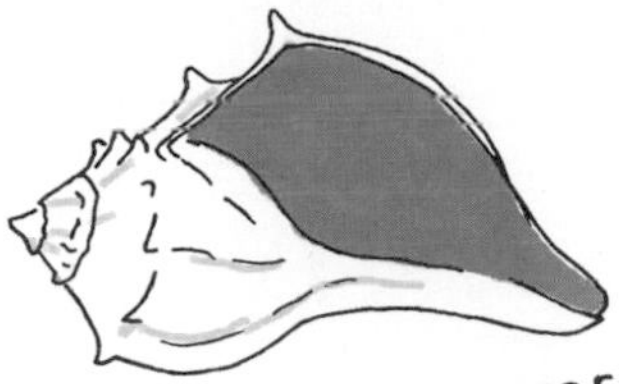

KNOBBED
WHELK

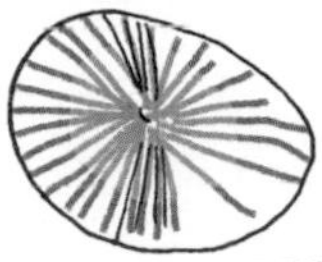

STRIPED
FALSE
LIMPET

Date:

Kind of shell:

Notes:

Date:

Kind of shell:

Notes:

Date:

Kind of shell:

Notes:

Date:

Kind of shell:

Notes:

SHELL-ABRATING PATTERNS

Shells come in many different shapes. On this page you will find some examples.

CONE HELMET CONCH MUREX WHELK CHITON WORM TUSK

AUGER RISSOID TOP OYSTER MOON SNAIL COWRY BUBBLE LIMPET

SLIPPER ABALONE SCALLOP COCKLE CLAM MUSSEL RAZOR

Look at the pattern of shells in each line. Figure out what shape should come next in the pattern and draw it on the blank.

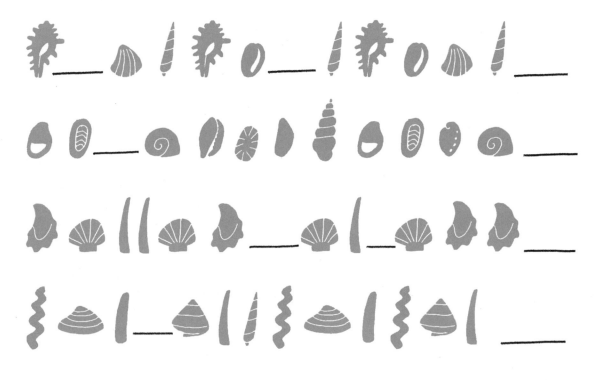

SEA SHAPES

In the art style Cubism, artists like Picasso created pictures of objects and people by using lots of small shapes, like squares and triangles. They then put these shapes together to make a bigger picture. This makes the artwork look like it's made out of lots of different pieces. Color in the shapes below with the color of the outline and see what creatures appear.

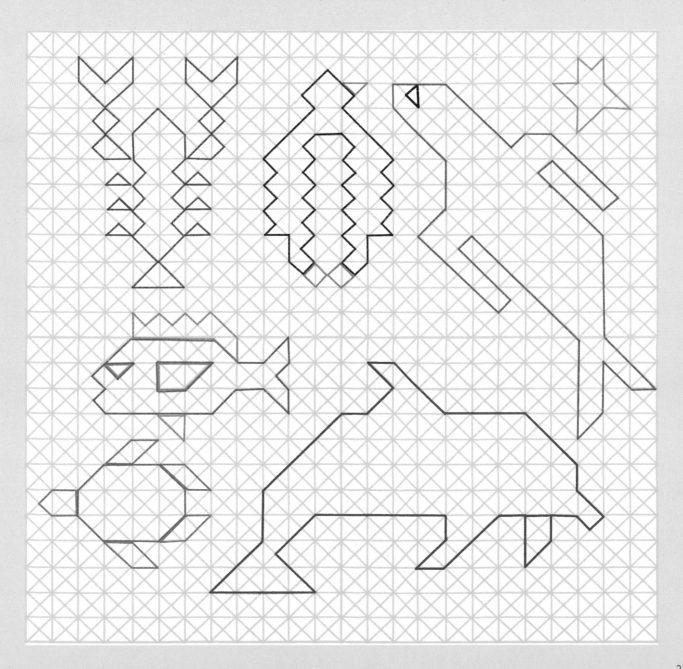

Animal Abilities

What kind of animal would you like to be? Read about the different abilities of each pair of animals. Draw a circle around the one you choose.

A moray eel has a second set of internal jaws for grasping and pulling in prey.

A black swallower has an expandable stomach and can consume fish twice its size and many times its weight.

A shark has a network of electroreceptive pores on its head that helps it sense the electrical fields of its prey.

A dolphin can emit high-pitched sounds and interpret the echoes to "see" its surroundings.

If injured by a predator, a sea star can regrow a missing limb.

A stingray has a venomous barb in its tail for defending itself.

Pistol shrimp hunt by snapping their claws shut with so much force that the sound stuns nearby prey.

Male narwhals use their long tusks to strike and stun small fish before eating them.

Sperm whales are up to 59 feet long. They have the largest brain of any animal on the planet.

Giant squids can be 33 feet long. They have the largest eyes of any living creature.

Or write here the ability you most want to have:

_____

MAKE IT:
FOLD AN ANGELFISH

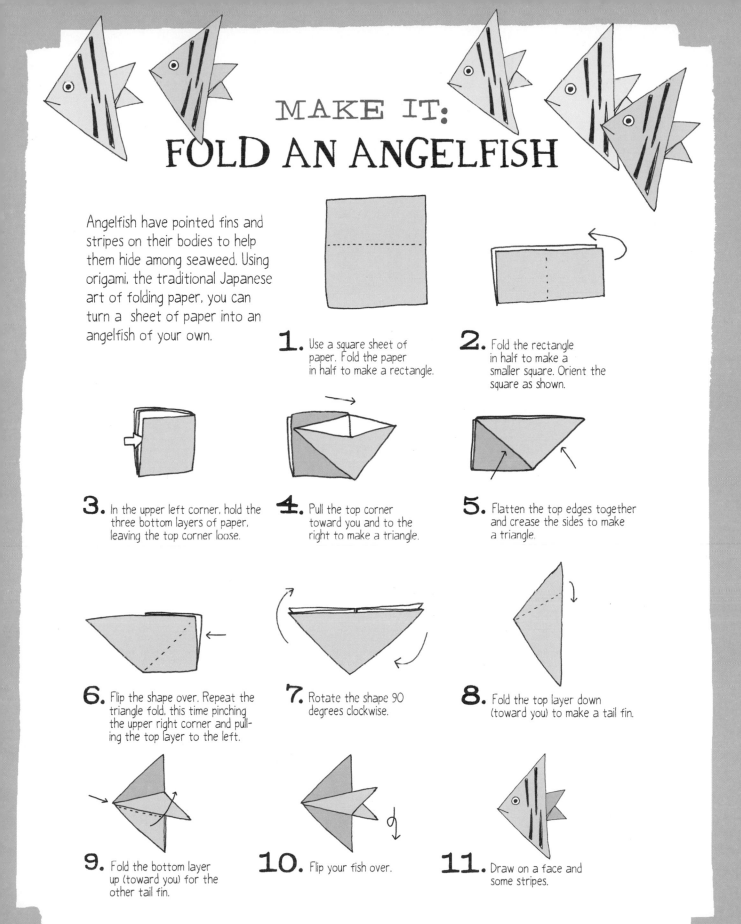

Angelfish have pointed fins and stripes on their bodies to help them hide among seaweed. Using origami, the traditional Japanese art of folding paper, you can turn a sheet of paper into an angelfish of your own.

1. Use a square sheet of paper. Fold the paper in half to make a rectangle.

2. Fold the rectangle in half to make a smaller square. Orient the square as shown.

3. In the upper left corner, hold the three bottom layers of paper, leaving the top corner loose.

4. Pull the top corner toward you and to the right to make a triangle.

5. Flatten the top edges together and crease the sides to make a triangle.

6. Flip the shape over. Repeat the triangle fold, this time pinching the upper right corner and pulling the top layer to the left.

7. Rotate the shape 90 degrees clockwise.

8. Fold the top layer down (toward you) to make a tail fin.

9. Fold the bottom layer up (toward you) for the other tail fin.

10. Flip your fish over.

11. Draw on a face and some stripes.

SHADES OF SEABIRDS

These birds are missing some of their colors. Read their descriptions below and then help them get their bright plummage back by coloring them correctly.

FRIGATEBIRD

Male frigatebirds inflate their bright red throat pouches to attract females.

BLUE-FOOTED BOOBY

The bluer a blue-footed booby's feet, the healthier the bird.

ROSEATE SPOONBILL

These large pink birds sweep their wide bills through the water to catch fish, insects, small crabs, and amphibians. Roseate spoonbills are pink because of the pigments in their food.

BROWN PELICAN

Brown pelicans have a foot-long bill and a 7-foot wingspan. During mating season, the feathers on their head turn bright yellow and those on their neck white, while the rest stays brown.

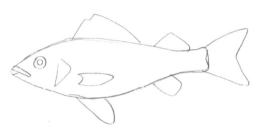

1. In pencil, sketch out a long oblong shape with a tapered end.

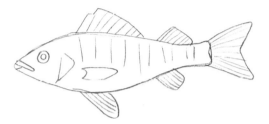

2. Add dorsal fins, a pelvic fin, an anal fin, and a caudal fin.

3. Add an eye, lips, gill cover, and pectoral fin.

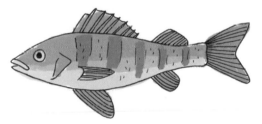

4. Add some lines to show texture on the fins and body.

5. Go over your lines in ink and erase the pencil lines.

6. Add color if you wish.

Now You Try ↲

FISH

The names of 18 seabirds and shorebirds are hidden in this word search. How many can you find? Search vertically, horizontally, diagonally, and backwards. Circle each one you find, then cross them off the list.

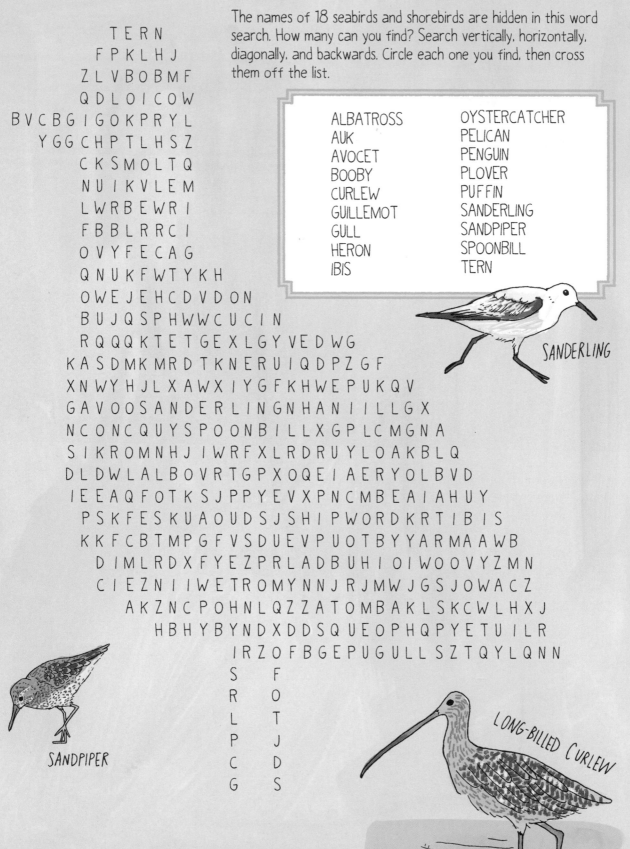

ALBATROSS   OYSTERCATCHER
AUK   PELICAN
AVOCET   PENGUIN
BOOBY   PLOVER
CURLEW   PUFFIN
GUILLEMOT   SANDERLING
GULL   SANDPIPER
HERON   SPOONBILL
IBIS   TERN

```
          T E R N
          F P K L H J
          Z L V B O B M F
          Q D L O I C O W
B V C B G I G O K P R Y L
  Y G G C H P T L H S Z
          C K S M O L T Q
          N U I K V L E M
          L W R B E W R I
          F B B L R R C I
          O V Y F E C A G
          Q N U K F W T Y K H
          O W E J E H C D V D O N
          B U J Q S P H W W C U C I N
          R Q Q Q K T E T G E X L G Y V E D W G
K A S D M K M R D T K N E R U I Q D P Z G F
X N W Y H J L X A W X I Y G F K H W E P U K Q V
G A V O O S A N D E R L I N G N H A N I I L L G X
N C O N C Q U Y S P O O N B I L L X G P L C M G N A
S I K R O M N H J I W R F X L R D R U Y L O A K B L Q
D L D W L A L B O V R T G P X O Q E I A E R Y O L B V D
I E E A Q F O T K S J P P Y E V X P N C M B E A I A H U Y
 P S K F E S K U A O U D S J S H I P W O R D K R T I B I S
 K K F C B T M P G F V S D U E V P U O T B Y Y A R M A A W B
   D I M L R D X F Y E Z P R L A D B U H I O I W O O V Y Z M N
   C I E Z N I I W E T R O M Y N N J R J M W J G S J O W A C Z
     A K Z N C P O H N L Q Z Z A T O M B A K L S K C W L H X J
       H B H Y B Y N D X D D S Q U E O P H Q P Y E T U I L R
         I R Z O F B G E P U G U L L S Z T Q Y L Q N N
       S       F
       R       O
       L       T
       P       J
       C       D
       G       S
```

SANDERLING

SANDPIPER

LONG-BILLED CURLEW

SWIM TO SAFETY

Can you help this seal swim through the waves?
Watch out for predators along the way!

MAKE IT:
UNDERWATER DRAWING

A wax-resist painting is made by doing a drawing on paper with crayon or oil pastel, then painting over it with watercolor. The wax repels the paint, allowing the design to show through. Draw an underwater scene on thick paper with your favorite sea creatures, coral, and seaweed. When you paint over your drawing with blue or green paint, your scene will come to life and appear to glow underwater.

What You'll Need:
- heavy white paper
- crayon or oil pastel
- cup of water
- watercolors

1. Use the crayon to draw an underwater scene. It might be hard to see if you use white crayon.

2. Wet the paintbrush thoroughly and mix the colors you want to use, imagining the blue and green colors of the ocean.

3. Paint over the entire drawing. Your crayon drawing should magically appear from under the paint.

The names of 27 sea creatures are hidden in this word search. How many can you find? Search vertically, horizontally, diagonally, and backwards. Circle each one you find, then cross it off the list.

```
                              W
                          E   S
                      N   U   N
                  O   R   K   O
              M   L   P   Y   I
          T K E A E S H A R K E                          D
        Y M L N W F T L F Z S R A H H                  G     X
      V D P E A H O E M T O N U S E S H H          C     S
      L I O L N N M R L L O B S T E R I V L Z      I   B H Z
      M U L C J W C T Z T E P M I L H L F W A B G C Y L E L
      Y Q L A O F E U U S E A L T W C Q M R P H C E E H I N B
    E S A N N C R I L E T U M P O N X B A A X W S F W D R A N
  Z T C R I I T J T P L T T N A A R N P L T C R T Q K L R E L
  Y S A V H H O I T E A Y P L R N E W Q C S O A D    C Q C G
  U B C J C P P Y U N H G F B E Z A R R N H C N        D A G
    A W S R L U A R G W Z I I P F E T J A D K          Z   F
    K A U O S C T U J D E M S B I H E O S                  K
      P B D G R L I U A I S Z H R S J E
      J R T O E N F R H P L W C S H
        V K G C H W R O B B U I
          P S L R J N Z A W
              S G V
              E P
              P
```

ANEMONE   MANATEE   SHARK
BARNACLE   NARWHAL   SHRIMP
CLAM   NUDIBRANCH   SPONGE
CRAB   OCTOPUS   SQUID
CUTTLEFISH   ORCA   STARFISH
DOLPHIN   OYSTER   TURTLE
JELLYFISH   PENGUIN   URCHIN
LIMPET   SCALLOP   WALRUS
LOBSTER   SEAHORSE   WHALE

THE DEEP SEA

The deepest, darkest depths of the ocean contain a thriving ecosystem of fascinating and mysterious creatures. Below are descriptions of some of the unique animals that inhabit the deep sea.

Draw a line from each description to the matching image.

PELICAN EEL

Also called the gulper eel because of its prominent hinged mouth, it attracts prey with pink and red bioluminescent cells at the end of its tail.

GOBLIN SHARK

This pinkish-skinned shark can extend its jaws out many inches when feeding.

PACIFIC VIPERFISH

Though scary-looking, this fish only reaches about one foot in length.

DUMBO OCTOPUS

Growing up to 5 feet long, it has been observed at depths of greater than 20,000 feet, deeper than any other octopus species. It propels itself with its earlike flaps, steering with its arms.

GIANT SPIDER CRAB

At up to 15 feet across, this species has the largest leg span of any crustacean.

Polar Poetry

An acrostic poem is a type of poem where the first letters of all the lines spell out a word or phrase, often the topic of the poem itself. Below is one about penguins.

Penguins waddle

Every day eating fish

Nestled in the snow

Great swimmers

Uniquely black and white

Ice all around

Nurturing their young

Now try writing your own poem about polar bears. Use the facts below to help you.

P _____

O _____

L _____

A _____

R _____

B _____

E _____

A _____

R _____

- Polar bears spend most of their lives on sea ice.

- They have strong claws and large furry paws for walking on frozen surfaces.

- They can swim for hundreds of miles.

- They hunt seals through holes in the ice.

- They roll in the snow to clean their fur.

- They have black skin, which absorbs heat from the sun.

- Mother bears dig dens in deep snowdrifts to have their tiny cubs.

C3　A1　A4　D2

B2　C4　A3　B1

D1　C2　C1　A2

B3　B4　D4　D3

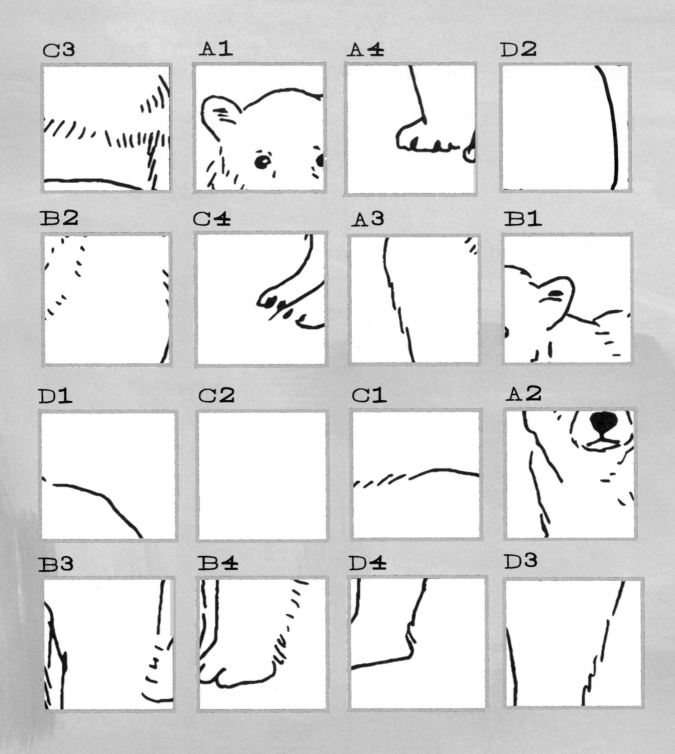

OFF THE GRID

Copy each square on the facing page into the correct space on the grid to reveal an animal that lives on Arctic sea ice.

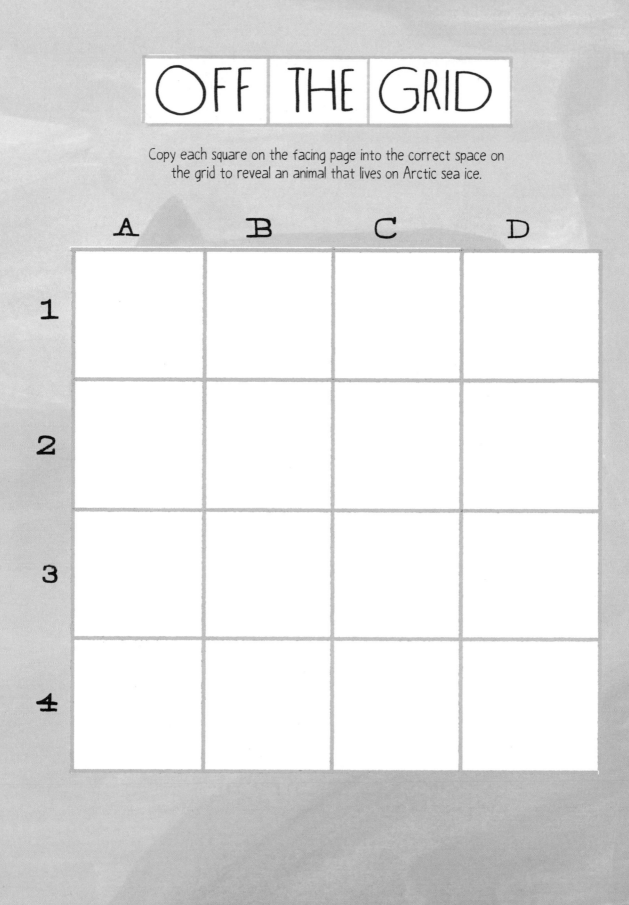

A JELLYFISH JAMBOREE

A group of jellyfish is called a swarm or a bloom. Large blooms may contain millions of jellyfish and cover 10 square miles!

Fill the page by drawing in the rest of the jellyfish in the bloom—or the sea turtle who might come to eat them.

Mammals of the Sea

A mammal is a warm-blooded animal that typically has fur or hair, feeds its young with milk, and gives birth to live young. Circle the mammals on this page.

NEW ZEALAND SCAMPI

YELLOWFIN TUNA

SPINNER DOLPHIN

EAGLE RAY

MOON SNAIL

RUDDY TURNSTONE

CUTTLEFISH

FLOUNDER

MANATEE

GALAPAGOS SEA LION

SPIDER DECORATOR CRAB

GREEN TURTLE

SCALLOP

LEOPARD SHARK

POLAR BEAR

PUT IN A GOOD WORD

Use the clues on this page to fill in words in the crossword.

Across

1. What people (and fish) do in the ocean
4. With this gear, divers can breathe underwater.
6. The largest ocean on Earth
8. A group of dolphins
10. Some of these creatures have stinging tentacles.
11. A male narwhal's elongated tooth
14. A type of seaweed that forms underwater forests
17. If you're lucky, you might find one inside an oyster.
18. Not a fish, but related to 21 Down
20. Shark with unique head shape that widens its field of vision
21. Fine particles of quartz, coral, or shells that cover a beach
22. These birds prey on baby sea turtles. They might grab your picnic, too!
25. Grows in many colors and shapes to form a reef
27. A shark may grow and lose 20,000 of these in its lifetime.
28. A huge, floating chunk broken from a glacier

Down

1. A meal for a polar bear
2. The percentage of the ocean floor that has been explored
3. A group of fish
5. Sounds like a vegetable but lives in the ocean
6. Harmful substances, such as trash, chemicals, and waste, that get into the ocean
7. Guiding light for ships
9. This creature can change the color and texture of its skin to hide from predators.
12. The largest animal that has ever lived on Earth
13. Underwater structures that provide habitat for fish, birds, mollusks, and other sea life
15. This bird has an 11-foot wingspan, the largest of any bird.
16. This type of crab might use a manmade container as its home.
19. The ____ ebbs and flows on beaches twice a day.
21. A sea creature with very large eyes, a beaklike mouth, and two long tentacles for grabbing prey
23. Colorful and iridescent flowerlike ocean animal
24. People used to harvest this plantlike animal for cleaning countertops and other household uses.
26. A rogue ____ can destroy ships and erode shorelines.

This tiny turtle got lost in the sand dunes while scrambling toward the sea with the other hatchlings. Can you help her find a way through the maze so she makes it safely to the water before a seagull eats her?

A SHELL LIKE ONE OTHER

Most of these shells appear just once, but three of them have doubles somewhere on the beach. Find the ones that appear twice and draw circles around them.

I SPY WITH MY LITTLE EYE...

Check off the plants, animals, and things you've seen with your own eyes.

sea star	oyster-catcher	scallop	seahorse
lighthouse	sea lion	beachgrass	a fin
pelican	clam hole in the sand	crab	gull
seaweed	a fish	a diver	barnacles
shark tooth	sea snails	sandpiper	buoy
clam	jellyfish	shrimp	shell

DIMPLE   KEYHOLE
DONUT

CORAL BLEACHING

Coral bleaching is when corals lose their bright colors and turn white because the water around them gets too warm, often due to climate change or pollution. Corals have tiny plants called algae living inside them that provide them with food and color. When the water gets too warm, the algae leave the corals, making the corals weak and vulnerable to disease, and they can die. Coral reefs are important for many creatures, so it's crucial to protect them and reduce the causes of coral bleaching.

Below is a drawing of a coral reef. In the bottom image, some of the coral has bleached and some of the fish are gone. Circle all the differences between the two drawings.

MAKE IT:
SWIMMING JELLYFISH

Jellyfish are fascinating creatures that can be found in oceans all around the world. With their flowing tentacles and graceful movements, they look like they're dancing underwater. Did you know that some jellyfish have tentacles that can be as long as a whale? Or that some jellyfish are so tiny, they can fit on the tip of your finger?

You can make your own jellyfish with just a paper plate and some streamers. Or make a whole school of them!

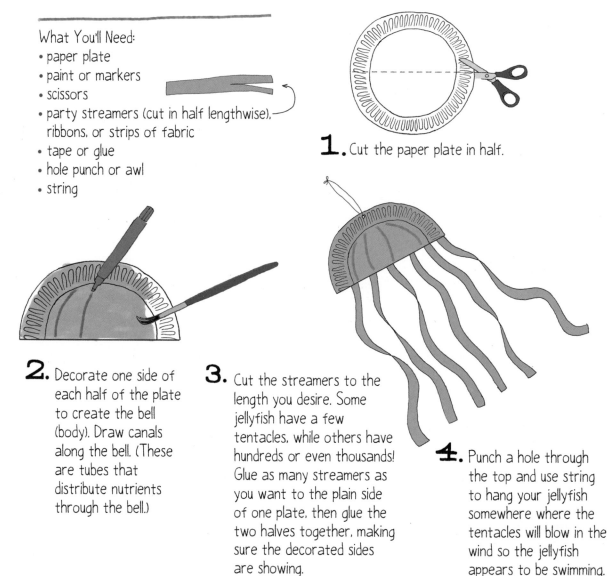

What You'll Need:
- paper plate
- paint or markers
- scissors
- party streamers (cut in half lengthwise), ribbons, or strips of fabric
- tape or glue
- hole punch or awl
- string

1. Cut the paper plate in half.

2. Decorate one side of each half of the plate to create the bell (body). Draw canals along the bell. (These are tubes that distribute nutrients through the bell.)

3. Cut the streamers to the length you desire. Some jellyfish have a few tentacles, while others have hundreds or even thousands! Glue as many streamers as you want to the plain side of one plate, then glue the two halves together, making sure the decorated sides are showing.

4. Punch a hole through the top and use string to hang your jellyfish somewhere where the tentacles will blow in the wind so the jellyfish appears to be swimming.

Lost at Sea

How many times do you see the word SEA? Look for it horizontally, vertically, and diagonally. Circle each one and make a mark on the tally sheet, then count the total.

A	E	S	A	E	A
E	S	A	S	S	E
A	E	S	E	A	S
S	E	A	A	E	E
S	A	E	S	S	A
A	E	S	A	E	E

TALLY:

TOTAL: _____

Can you guess these words that start with SEA?

SEA _ _ _ _ _ _   On the menu at many coastal restaurants

SEA _ _ _ _ _   A large bird with a loud call

SEA _ _ _ _ _ _   Aircraft that takes off and lands on water

SEA _ _ _ _ _   Plant that provides habitat for many creatures

KELP ME EXPLORE

Pretend you are doing a deep dive. Find the details in circles on the sides of these pages in the kelp forest and circle them.

ROCKFISH

GIANT KELP

PACIFIC SEA NETTLE

LEOPARD SHARK

SEA OTTER

OPALEYE

KELP
CRAB

CALIFORNIA
SHEEPHEAD

GIANT
SEA
BASS

RED SEA
URCHIN

HALFWAY THERE

Look at the patterns of the fish, coral, and nudibranch below. Color in the blank parts by matching the color and pattern of the other half.

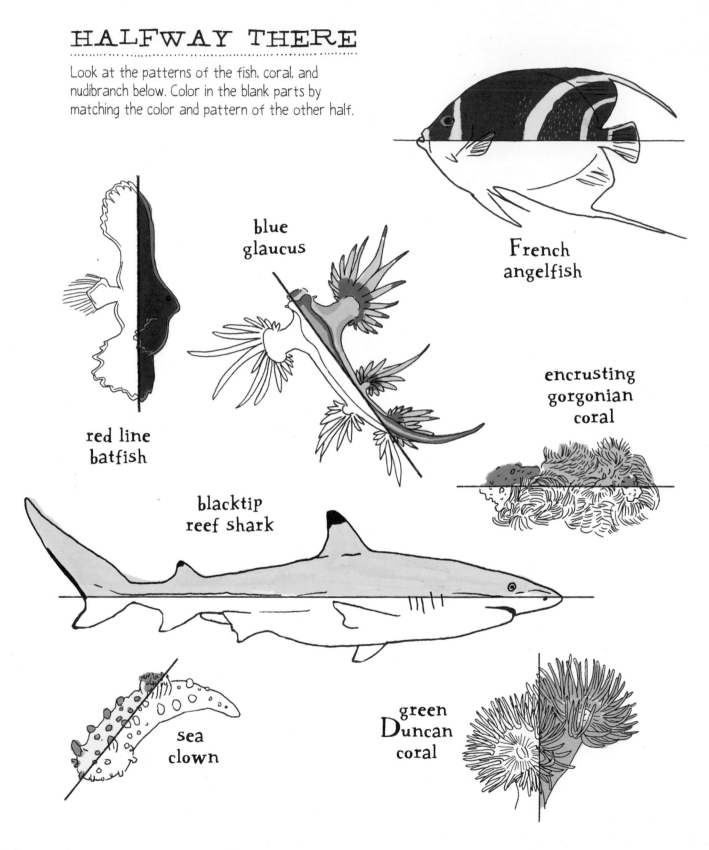

French angelfish

blue glaucus

red line batfish

encrusting gorgonian coral

blacktip reef shark

sea clown

green Duncan coral

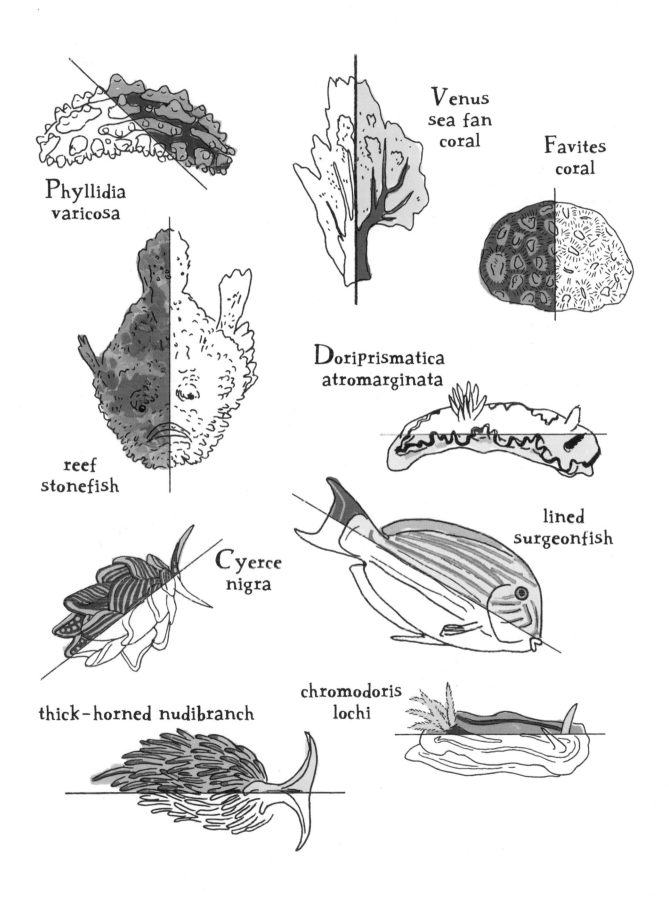

Phyllidia
varicosa

Venus
sea fan
coral

Favites
coral

reef
stonefish

Doriprismatica
atromarginata

lined
surgeonfish

Cyerce
nigra

thick-horned nudibranch

chromodoris
lochi

COLORFUL CORAL

Finish writing the names of the corals, using the color as a clue. Then unscramble the circled letters to find the name of the yellow coral.

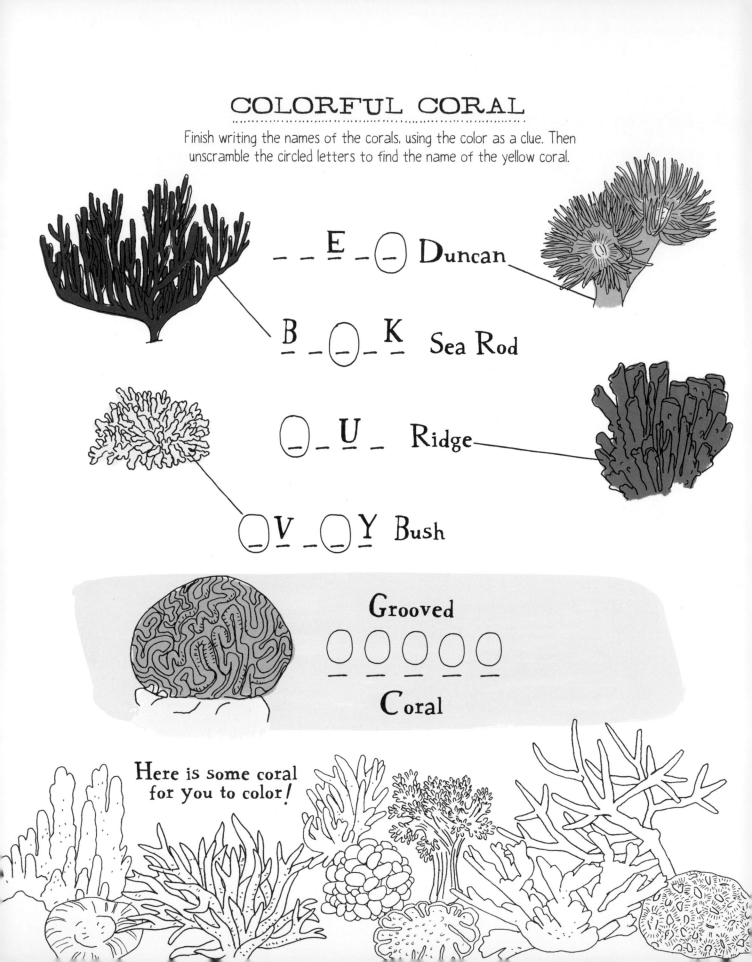

_ _ E _ _(_) Duncan

B _ _(_)_ K Sea Rod

(_)_ U _ Ridge

(_) V _(_) Y Bush

Grooved

(◯) (◯) (◯) (◯) (◯)
_ _ _ _ _

Coral

Here is some coral for you to color!

MANATEE LANES

Follow each manatee on its winding journey. When you reach the
end, write the correct number on the corresponding manatee.

SHADOW QUEST

Can you figure out what these sea creatures are from their shadow? Use the word bank below to help you label each animal.

roosterfish
giant squid
manatee
swordfish
seahorse
narwhal
manta ray

spinner dolphin
anglerfish
octopus
great white shark
yellowfin tuna
jellyfish
shrimp

Lighthouses

Lighthouses emit a powerful beam of light to aid vessels in avoiding rocks and other dangers near shore. These structures can be found all over the world, and each one has its own unique design, shape, and color. Some lighthouses are tall and slender, while others are short and stout. Some are painted with bold stripes. Some feature decorative details such as cupolas and balconies.

The concentrated beam of light, like the one coming from the lighthouse at top left, can be seen from a great distance and helps ships to navigate safely at night and in storms.

Color in a beam of light coming from each of the other lighthouses.

Now try designing your own lighthouse on the shoreline.

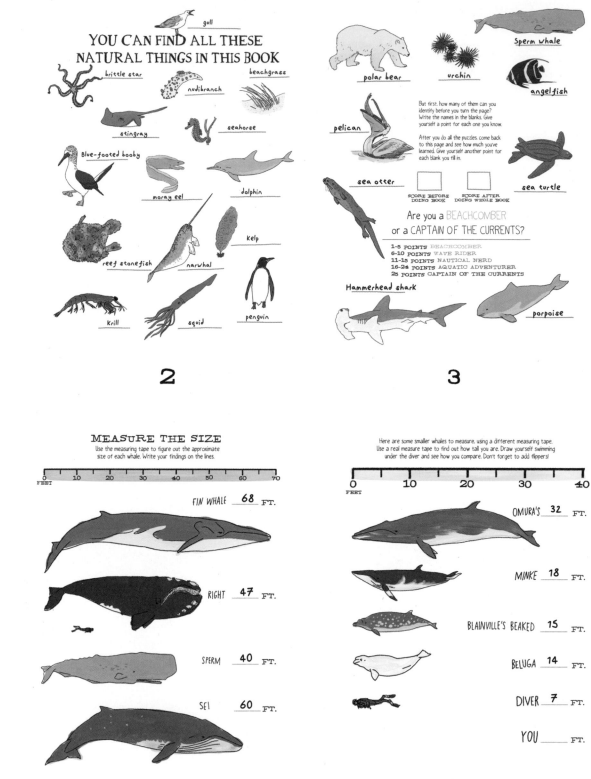

ANSWER KEY

2

YOU CAN FIND ALL THESE NATURAL THINGS IN THIS BOOK

gull

brittle star

nudibranch

beachgrass

stingray

seahorse

Blue-footed booby

moray eel

dolphin

reef stonefish

narwhal

kelp

krill

squid

penguin

3

polar bear

urchin

Sperm whale

angelfish

pelican

But first, how many of them can you identify before you turn the page? Write the names in the blanks. Give yourself a point for each one you know.

After you do all the puzzles, come back to this page and see how much you've learned. Give yourself another point for each blank you fill in.

sea otter

sea turtle

SCORE BEFORE DOING BOOK

SCORE AFTER DOING WHOLE BOOK

Are you a BEACHCOMBER or a CAPTAIN OF THE CURRENTS?

1-5 POINTS BEACHCOMBER
6-10 POINTS WAVE RIDER
11-15 POINTS NAUTICAL NERD
16-24 POINTS AQUATIC ADVENTURER
25 POINTS CAPTAIN OF THE CURRENTS

Hammerhead shark

porpoise

4

MEASURE THE SIZE

Use the measuring tape to figure out the approximate size of each whale. Write your findings on the lines.

0 10 20 30 40 50 60 70
FEET

FIN WHALE **68** FT.

RIGHT **47** FT.

SPERM **40** FT.

SEI **60** FT.

5

Here are some smaller whales to measure, using a different measuring tape. Use a real measure tape to find out how tall you are. Draw yourself swimming under the diver and see how you compare. Don't forget to add flippers!

0 10 20 30 40
FEET

OMURA'S **32** FT.

MINKE **18** FT.

BLAINVILLE'S BEAKED **15** FT.

BELUGA **14** FT.

DIVER **7** FT.

YOU _____ FT.

Dolphin-ately Different

Dolphins and porpoises may look similar but there are some small differences when you look closely. See if you can find them and label the drawing with the descriptive words from the box below.

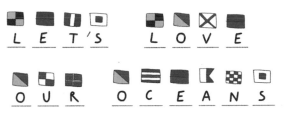

curved dorsal fin
long beak
slender body
cone-shaped teeth

DOLPHIN

long beak   triangular dorsal fin   spade-shaped teeth   slender body
small mouth   curved dorsal fin   cone-shaped teeth   round body

triangular dorsal fin
small mouth
round body
spade-shaped teeth

PORPOISE

6

SECRET CODE

Nautical signal flags are used internationally for ship-to-ship communication. Each flag has a specific meaning. Can you decipher the coded message below using these flags?

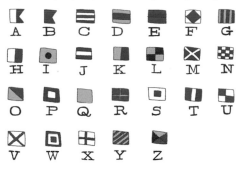

A B C D E F G
H I J K L M N
O P Q R S T U
V W X Y Z

WHAT'S THE MESSAGE?

L E T ' S   L O V E

O U R   O C E A N S

9

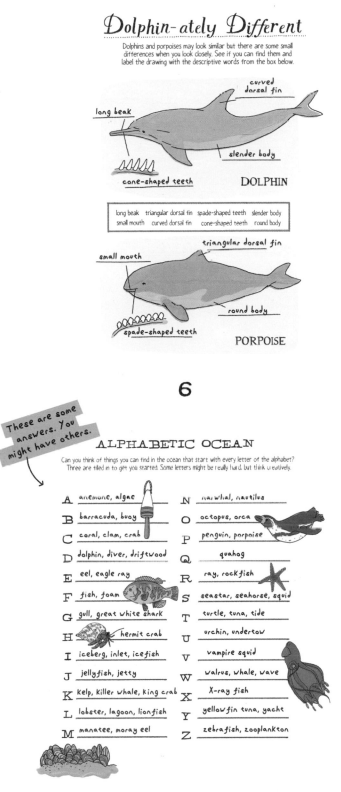

These are some answers. You might have others.

ALPHABETIC OCEAN

Can you think of things you can find in the ocean that start with every letter of the alphabet? Three are filled in to get you started. Some letters might be really hard, but think creatively.

A anemone, algae
B barracuda, buoy
C coral, clam, crab
D dolphin, diver, driftwood
E eel, eagle ray
F fish, foam
G gull, great white shark
H hermit crab
I iceberg, inlet, icefish
J jellyfish, jetty
K kelp, killer whale, king crab
L lobster, lagoon, lionfish
M manatee, moray eel
N narwhal, nautilus
O octopus, orca
P penguin, porpoise
Q quahog
R ray, rockfish
S seastar, seahorse, squid
T turtle, tuna, tide
U urchin, undertow
V vampire squid
W walrus, whale, wave
X X-ray fish
Y yellowfin tuna, yacht
Z zebrafish, zooplankton

10

ANATOMY OF AN OCTOPUS

Draw the number of each part in the corresponding line next to the description.

2 **arm** flexible appendage covered in suckers
4 **siphon** for breathing and propulsion through water
3 **sucker** for gripping prey
5 **mantle** bag-like body
1 **eye** has a rectangular pupil

11

TIDAL ZONE ECOSYSTEM

Without flipping back to the previous page, how many sea creatures can you name?

limpet
brittle star
striped shore crab
sea cucumber
turban snail
anemone
mussels
opaleye fish

sea urchins
gull
hermit crab
barnacles
seaweed
sponge
sea star

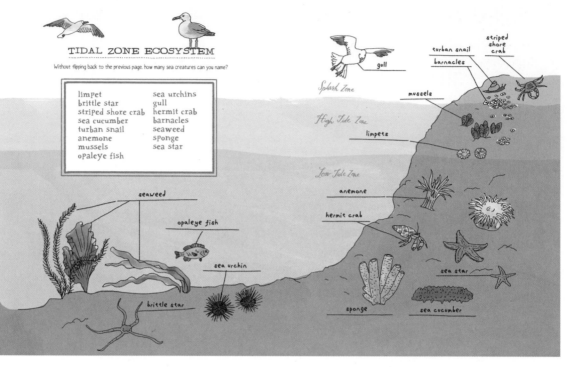

14

15

FEELING CRABBY?

Fill in the 4-by-4 grid so that all the letters of the word C-R-A-B appear only once in each row and once in each column.

B	A	R	C
R	C	B	A
C	R	A	B
A	B	C	R

Crabs are crustaceans that have hard exoskeletons and 10 legs, including their claws. These crabs are missing some legs and claws. Can you draw the missing ones to match?

SEA CREATURE SCRAMBLER

Can you unscramble the letters to figure out the names of these ocean crawlers? Write the names in the spaces below each one.

rilkl
k r i l l

qudis
s q u i d

aes tsra
s e a s t a r

wons brca
s n o w c r a b

reblost
l o b s t e r

optcosu
o c t o p u s

oonm nasil
m o o n s n a i l

clopsal
s c a l l o p

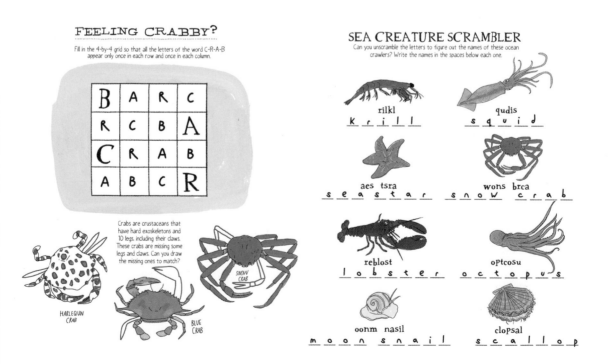

HARLEQUIN CRAB

BLUE CRAB

SNOW CRAB

17

19

SHELL-ABRATING PATTERNS

Shells come in many different shapes. On this page you will find some examples

CONE HELMET CONCH MUREX WHELK CHITON WORM TUSK

AUGER RISSOID TOP OYSTER MOON SNAIL COWRY BUBBLE LIMPET

SLIPPER ABALONE SCALLOP COCKLE CLAM MUSSEL RAZOR

Look at the pattern of shells in each line. Figure out what shape should come next in the pattern and draw it on the blank.

SEA SHAPES

In the art style Cubism, artists like Picasso created pictures of objects and people by using lots of small shapes, like squares and triangles. They then put these shapes together to make a bigger picture. This makes the artwork look like it's made out of lots of different pieces. Color in the shapes with the color of the outline and see what creatures appear.

22

23

SHADES OF SEABIRDS

These birds are missing some of their colors. Read their descriptions below and then help them get their bright plumage back by coloring them correctly.

FRIGATEBIRD

Male frigatebirds inflate their bright red throat pouches to attract females.

BLUE-FOOTED BOOBY

The bluer a blue-footed booby's feet, the healthier the bird.

ROSEATE SPOONBILL

These large pink birds sweep their wide bills through the water to catch fish, insects, small crabs, and amphibians. Roseate spoonbills are pink because of the pigments in their food.

BROWN PELICAN

Brown pelicans have a foot-long bill and a 7-foot wingspan. During mating season, the feathers on their head turn bright yellow and those on their neck white, while the rest stays brown.

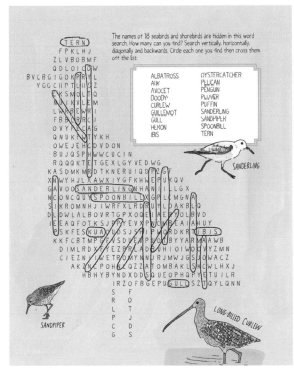

The names of 18 seabirds and shorebirds are hidden in this word search. How many can you find? Search vertically, horizontally, diagonally and backwards. Circle each one you find then cross them off the list.

ALBATROSS	OYSTERCATCHER
AUK	PELICAN
AVOCET	PENGUIN
BOOBY	PLOVER
CURLEW	PUFFIN
GUILLEMOT	SANDERLING
GULL	SANDPIPER
HERON	SPOONBILL
IBIS	TERN

26

28

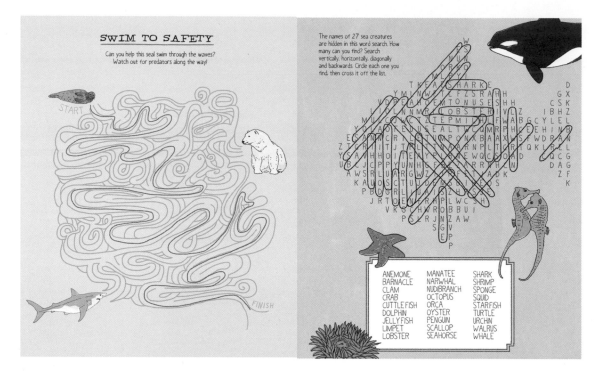

SWIM TO SAFETY

Can you help this seal swim through the waves?
Watch out for predators along the way!

START

FINISH

The names of 27 sea creatures
are hidden in this word search. How
many can you find? Search
vertically, horizontally, diagonally
and backwards. Circle each one you
find, then cross it off the list.

ANEMONE	MANATEE	SHARK
BARNACLE	NARWHAL	SHRIMP
CLAM	NUDIBRANCH	SPONGE
CRAB	OCTOPUS	SQUID
CUTTLEFISH	ORCA	STARFISH
DOLPHIN	OYSTER	TURTLE
JELLYFISH	PENGUIN	URCHIN
LIMPET	SCALLOP	WALRUS
LOBSTER	SEAHORSE	WHALE

29

31

THE DEEP SEA

The deepest, darkest depths of the ocean contain a thriving ecosystem of fascinating and mysterious
creatures. Below are descriptions of some of the unique animals that inhabit the deep sea.

Draw a line from each description to the matching image.

PELICAN EEL

Also called the gulper eel
because of its prominent hinged
mouth, it attracts prey with
pink and red bioluminescent
cells at the end of its tail.

GOBLIN SHARK

This pinkish-skinned shark can
extend its jaws out many inches
when feeding.

PACIFIC VIPERFISH

Though scary looking, this fish only
reaches about one foot in length.

DUMBO OCTOPUS

Growing up to 5 feet long, it has been
observed at depths of greater than
20,000 feet, deeper than any other
octopus species. It propels itself with its
ear-like flaps, steering with its arms.

GIANT SPIDER CRAB

At up to 15 feet across, this
species has the largest leg span
of any crustacean.

OFF THE GRID

Copy each square on the facing page into the correct space on
the grid to reveal an animal that lives on Arctic sea ice.

A   B   C   D

1

2

3

4

32

34

37

39

40

A SHELL LIKE ONE OTHER

Most of these shells appear just once, but three of them have doubles somewhere on the beach. Find the ones that appear twice and draw circles around them.

41

CORAL BLEACHING

Coral bleaching is when corals lose their bright colors and turn white because the water around them gets too warm, often due to climate change or pollution. Corals have tiny plants called algae living inside them that provide them with food and color. When the water gets too warm, the algae leave the corals, making the corals weak and vulnerable to disease, and they can die. Coral reefs are important for many creatures, so it's crucial to protect them and reduce the causes of coral bleaching.

Below is a drawing of a coral reef. In the bottom image, some of the coral has bleached and some of the fish are gone. Circle all the differences between the two drawings.

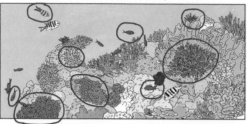

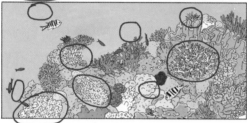

43

Lost at Sea

How many times do you see the word SEA? Look for it horizontally, vertically, backwards and diagonally. Circle each one and make a mark on the tally sheet, then count the total.

TALLY:

TOTAL: **13**

Can you guess these words that start with SEA?

SEA **FOOD**   On the menu at many coastal restaurants

SEA **GULL**   A large bird with a loud call

SEA **PLANE**   Aircraft that takes off and lands on water

SEA **WEED**   Plant that provides habitat for many creatures

45

KELP ME EXPLORE

Pretend you are doing a deep dive. Find the details in circles on the sides of these pages in the kelp forest and circle them.

46   **47**

COLORFUL CORAL

Finish writing the names of the corals, using the color as a clue. Then unscramble the circled letters to find the name of the yellow coral.

G R E E N Duncan

B L A C K Sea Rod

B L U E Ridge

I V O R Y Bush

Grooved B R A I N Coral

Here is some coral for you to color!

MANATEE LANES

Follow each manatee on its winding journey. When you reach the end, write the correct number on the corresponding manatee.

50

51

SHADOW QUEST

Can you figure out what these sea creatures are from their shadow? Use the word bank below to help you label each animal.

roosterfish
giant squid
manatee
swordfish
seahorse
narwhal
manta ray

spinner dolphin
anglerfish
octopus
great white shark
yellowfin tuna
jellyfish
shrimp

great white shark

spinner dolphin

manta ray

jellyfish

narwhal

swordfish

manatee

seahorse

giant squid

shrimp

anglerfish

yellowfin tuna

roosterfish

octopus

52

53

Storey books are available at special discounts when purchased in bulk for premiums and sales promotions as well as for fund-raising or educational use. Special editions or book excerpts can also be created to specification. For details, please send an email to special.markets@hbgusa.com.

Storey Publishing
210 MASS MoCA Way
North Adams, MA 01247
storey.com

Storey Publishing is an imprint of Workman Publishing, a division of Hachette Book Group, Inc., 1290 Avenue of the Americas, New York, NY 10104

Distributed in Europe by Hachette Livre, 58 rue Jean Bleuzen, 92 178 Vanves Cedex, France
Distributed in the United Kingdom by Hachette Book Group, UK, Carmelite House, 50 Victoria Embankment, London EC4Y 0DZ

ISBN: 978-1-63586-778-7 (Paperback)

Printed in China through Asia Pacific Offset on paper from responsible sources
10 9 8 7 6 5 4 3 2 1

Library of Congress Cataloging-in-Publication Data on file